WORD SMASH

By
Kayden Grace Swan

DEDICATED TO THE...

Parents who had to become teachers.

Teachers who were telling the truth all along.

Students who thought school being closed was
going to be fun!

ABOUT THE BOOK...

Even as a 12-year-old, I know that Quarantine 2020 will go down as the biggest **KIDTASTROPHE** in history. Locked indoors, no friends in person, virtual homeschool, disinfectant and masks everywhere and toilet paper nowhere. And the worst part, nonstop boredom. It's been tough.

During one of my online vocabulary lessons, I learned that complex compound words are just words smashed together to make another word. I realized I'd been making up my own humorous smashed words since I was young. I thought it would be fun to create a **FICTIONARY** book of my favorite smashed words that shared my experiences during the **BORINTINE**.

With the help of my super creative mom, we brought in my friend Ari to draw cartoons to illustrate the many hilarious situations my words describe. The end result is an entertaining look into my **CONFABULOUS** way of expressing myself.

I hope you enjoyed this book and that it makes you laugh in these **UNFANORMAL** times. And just remember, we will forget the craziness of 2020 one day, just like we forget to plug in our phones at night.

Kayden S

 [soh-shuhl-mis-tuhn-sing]

when you are lost and lacking your friends due to social distancing.

"

I'm totally *SOCIALMISSTANCING* hanging out with all my friends.

"

PROCRASTICHORES

 [proh-kras-tuh-chohrs]

any delayed, unpleasant, mandatory tasks around the house. Usually put off until another day or time at the risk of losing your phone.

 I have way more important things to do than PROCRASTICHORES.

ACCICURSE

[ak-si-kurs]

to accidently use profanity, curse or swear in front of your parents or anyone that might snitch to your parents.

> " I couldn't help but to **ACCICURSE** when I stepped on that toy block. "

PROFAMITY

 [pruh-fam-i-tee]

when your family is completely okay using inappropriate language around younger family members, usually followed by, "You didn't hear that."

 Game night at my house always involves some PROFAMITY.

ANNOYBLINGS

[uh-noib-lings]

a brother or sister who continuously disturbs or bothers you and your friends to the point of ragittation.

> **My Mom always wants me to play with my younger ANNOYBLINGS.**

PARENTOID

[pair-uhn-toid]

a parent who has an extreme distrust or suspicion about what their child is doing, specifically in regards to their phone.

> "My Mom is so *PARENTOID* she barely lets my little brother outside."

 [broh-foo-luh-ree]

acts of silly, unintelligent behavior or henanagains performed by your brother.

> " I am so tired of the constant **BROFOOLERY** that he does every single day. "

 *[in-ter-naht]*

a vast computer network where you should be able to find information on almost anything, but you fail to get connected to it.

 My *INTERNOT* is taking forever to play one single video.

 *[hee-nan-uh-geynz]*

a mischievous or prankish trick done by a young man who lacks maturity.

" It is so cute when he tries to get my attention with *HENANAGAINS*. "

 [snap-tok-a-gram]

when you successfully use one post across three of your favorite social media platforms.

" I'm going to **SNAPTOKAGRAM** this new filter on all my pictures. "

 *[mom-lar-kee]*

when your Mom goes on and on with exaggerated or foolish talk, usually intended to humomilate you.

> " I hope everyone knows this is all just a bunch of *MOMLARKEY*. "

 [dad-ber-gast-uhd]

when you're overcome with surprise and bewilderment and downright astounded by something your Father said in an effort to be cool.

" I was totally *DADBERGASTED* when he said his business meeting was lit. "

 *[seel-tyhm]*

time spent in face-to-ceiling contact with someone over a video calling service.

> **I've been on this CEILTIME call for hours watching his fan spin around.**

 *[loud-ch-ing]*

the overexaggeration of chewing usually done with an open mouth. Otherwise known as smacking.

" He took handfuls of chips and was *LOUDCHING* one right after the other. "

 [ha-chee-ing-urs]

the brightly-colored flaming orange residue left behind after devouring an entire bag of snacks.

> **Do not get near my new white outfit with those HACHEEINGERS of yours.**

 [skruhmp-a-lish-uhs]

a very pleasing snack or food item that looks, smells and tastes delictable.

> The chocolate chip cookies fresh out of the oven are so *SCRUMPALICIOUS*.

 [frahy-nch-us

thin strips of deep-fried potatoes that are doused in a creamy buttermilk dipping sauce.

 I'll take a hamburger and a large order of **FRYNCHES**, please.

NOCTEXTURNAL

 [nok-teks-turnl]

the act of returning text messages only during the night. Usually results in someone feeling textglected.

> **My friends are all such NOCTEXTURNAL creatures during sleepovers.**

 [muhl-tee-vahys]

to successfully operate two or more electronic or mechanical inventions simultaneously.

Some days I can *MULTIVISE* like a dextrous octopus.

KRANCH

[k-ranch]

the delictable sauce mixture of ketchup and ranch dressing. Preferably used on fries, chicken and pizza.

> Please make my burger with extra **KRANCH** and cheese.

KIFTED

[kif-tid]

when your feline pet makes a loving gesture of presenting you with various critters from outside.

> My kitty looked so sad after she **KIFTED** me and I ran.

 *[uhn-fuh-nawr-muhl]*

The current state of feeling different; unaccustomed; unusual or strange after some dramatic change has transpired.

> " Everything going on right now is all so very *UNFANORMAL*. "

CONZOOMED

[kuhn-zoom-d]

to be completely absorbed and occupied all day by online video classes.

> " I can't even text my friends today because I've been so *CONZOOMED*. "

  [chaw-koh-muh]

a state of prolonged unconsciousness, due to the over consumption of any sweet and gooey deliciousness.

" When you wake up from a *CHOCOMMA* you are always thirsty. "

 [hyoo-mom-ee-leyt]

when your Mother tells childhood
memories that cause a painful loss of
pride, self-respect or dignity, in front of
all your friends.

She always tries to HUMOMILATE me with the nickel story.

 [mak-fahy]

when your wireless connectivity to the internet is as weak as that of a local fast food restaurant.

" I can barely check my email on this *MCFI*. "

 [feyk-fesh-uhn]

an untrue acceptance of guilt or responsibility for someone elses lapse of judgment. Also known as taking one for the team.

" My *FAKEFESSION* to her was totally believable. "

 [toh-miz-uh-ree]

the wretched feeling when one of the digits of the human foot accidentally strikes against a projecting object.

" How can you laugh at someone in *TOEMISERY* ? "

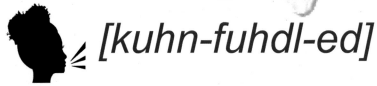 *[kuhn-fuhdl-ed]*

to become perplexed or bewildered by statements or arguments that make no sense.

> She has me so *CONFUDDLED* by saying that she is not crushing on him.

  [klohz-tas-truh-fee]

any unfortunate mishap or epic failure regarding the perfect outfit, otherwise known as a fashion fiasco.

> **These stripes and plaids are causing me to have a major CLOTHESTASTROPHY.**

CRIEND

[kr-end]

an unpredictable, nonconforming oddball buddy with intensely enthusiastic and excited feelings.

> Don't mind my **CRIEND** she always laughs at my jokes like that.

 *[i-pree-ohn]*

the previously owned cell phone that you receive once one of your parents gets an upgrade. Usually comes without an original charger or headphones.

> "
> Mom, please remove your contacts from my "new" *IPREOWN*.
> "

 *[teech-er-uhs]*

when your trust is broken by an instructor. Usually takes place during a parent teacher conference.

> Her *TEACHEROUS* attack on my book report was unnecessary, IMO.

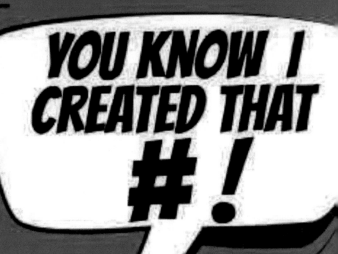

[hash-hohl]

a mean person who steals the hashtag you originated and spent a year developing.

" That was a real *HASHOLE* move especially when you don't even follow me. "

SNACKDASHERY

 [snak-dash-uh-ree]

an area in your bedroom that resembles a retail dealer in tasty morsels, such as candy, cookies, chips and soda.

"I prepared a whole **SNACKDASHERY** for the sleepover."

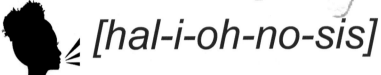 *[hal-i-oh-no-sis]*

the moment you realize you have offensive-smelling breath, usually in the morning after enjoying your snackdashery the night before.

> **Many people who have *HALIOHNOSIS* do not even know it.**

TEXGLECTED

[teks-glekt-id]

when your text messages are disregarded otherwise known as "left on read." Usually done by your noctexturnal friends.

> " He **TEXGLECTED** me all day and then sent me an emoji at midnight. "

 *[fren-gee]*

awkward, uncomfortable and/or
embarassing buddy behavior.

" Did you see how *FRIENGY*
she started acting when
the party started? "

[bruhsh]

when your friends have a crush for someone they know they cannot have a relationship with because it's your brother.

> She had an awful **BRUHSH** on him during middle school.

[skahr-tl-d]

to disturb or agitate suddenly as by surprise or alarm simultaneously causing fear or terror. Usually a spider is involved.

> She **SCARTLED** the mess out of me when she did that prank.

PIZAMISHED

 *[pee-zam-isht]*

when you are extremely hungry and only a flat, open-faced baked pie of Italian origin can satisfy you.

" We always get *PIZAMISHED* during sleepovers at two in the morning. "

[grah-muh-uhs-ing]

when your Grandmother complains nonstop especially about something relatively unimportant. Usually takes place in front of your friends.

> **Eating all your food will usually stop the *GRAMUSSING*.**

RAGITTATED

[reyj-i-tey-tid]

angered, provoked, or annoyed to the point of rage. Usually takes place when your Mom asks you to do something in the middle of an online game.

"I get so *RAGITTATED* when my Mom says I can't hang out with my friends."

 [cuhn-fuh-sish-uhs]

the state of being unsure and especially finding doubt in your thoughts or feelings.

" I am completely **CONFUSCIOUS** about the comment she just made. "

GUFAWART

[guh-fahrt]

a loud, unrestrained burst of laughter directly followed by an unexpected release of gas sounding like a horn or whistle.

> My *GUFAWART* was so loud it shocked everyone around me.

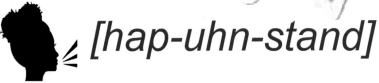 *[hap-uhn-stand]*

when you accidently hold a perfect handstand when you meant to do a front walk over.

> I held that *HAPPENSTAND* for **20** seconds and landed into a split.

 [grah-muh-ged-n]

when your Grandmother comes at you with great and crucial conflict, usually followed by getting on her last nerve.

"

Stop screaming so loud or it's about to be GRAMMAGEDDON up in here.

"

ABOUT THE AUTHOR...

KAYDEN SWAN has always exuded a creative spirit with a combination of panache and exuberance. At age nine she launched **@KAYDENSTYLE**, an Instagram account where she shares her eclectic fashion sense. Simultaneously, she created the **MADSLIMENTIST** YouTube channel where Kayden expresses her comedic abilities paired with the slime-making trend.

SHOUT OUTS... Thank you to my Mom for allowing me to always be creative. To my Dad for making me appreciate reading. To my Auntie Itram for always correcting my grammar and teaching me a fondness for language. And to my entire family and friends for loving my goofiness.

ABOUT THE ILLUSTRATOR...

ARI GREENIDGE is an amazingly talented illustrator. In 2018 Ari, an 18-year-old high school student, designed and hand painted a pair of custom sneakers, capturing the true essence of kayden Style. It was during that amazing artistic process that the undeniable connection these two young creatives share was forever established. The moment Kayden decided to write WORD SMASH she knew Ari could be the only illustrator to bring it all to life.